Recorder Trios
from the Beginning

John Pitts

Ensemble playing brings pleasure to all involved, and with it an incentive to learn new notes and rhythms in order to succeed. Incidental development of listening skills and concentration is also required for success.

This collection of 14 mixed recorder trios is suitable for either three players or group ensembles. It features a wide range of repertoire which includes classical favourites, folk songs, spirituals, blues, a Christmas medley and Latin American and Caribbean items, together with original pieces by John Pitts.

The trios feature three different recorder groupings, with the music grouped into corresponding sections:

2 descants and treble
descant and 2 trebles (optional tenor can replace 2nd treble)
descant, treble and tenor

Within each section the music is graded so far as possible, both in range of notes (pitches) included and level of difficulty.

In each piece the musical interest is generally divided between all three instruments, so that all players have the opportunity to play the main tune.

In keeping with the 'repertoire' nature of the book, only a minimum of help or explanation is given. Where more help is required it is best to refer to the appropriate pages of the teaching scheme *Recorder from the Beginning*.

CHESTER MUSIC

Contents

2 descants and treble:

Little David Play On Your Harp	4
La Donna È Mobile	6
Rondo K.213	9
Beckett Blues	12
Go Down, Moses	16
Christmas Spirituals	18

descant and 2 trebles: (or descant, treble and tenor)

The Gospel Train	22
St Anthony Chorale	24
An Eriskay Love Lilt	26
Yellow Bird Calypso	28

descant, treble and tenor:

Las Heras Beguine	32
American Patrol	36
Calypso Carnival	40
Scott Joplin In Concert	44

Little David Play On Your Harp   Spiritual

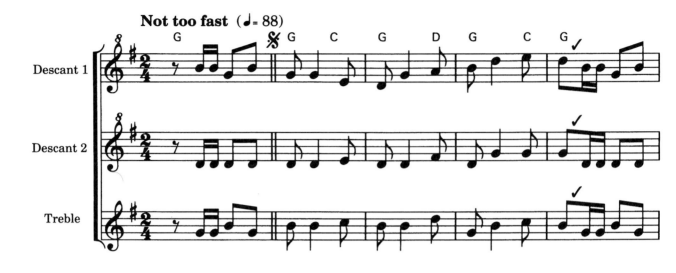

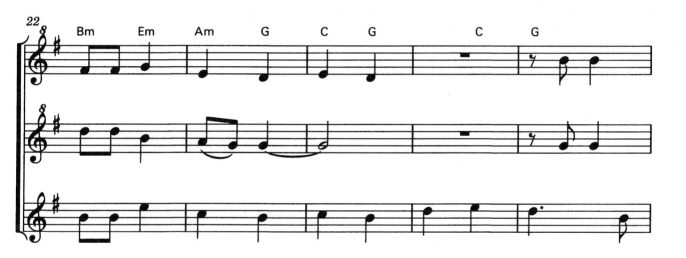

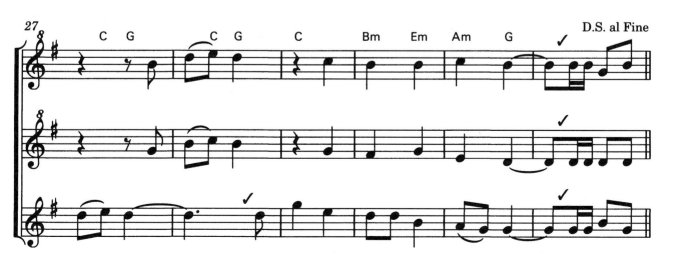

5

La Donna È Mobile (from Rigoletto)   Verdi

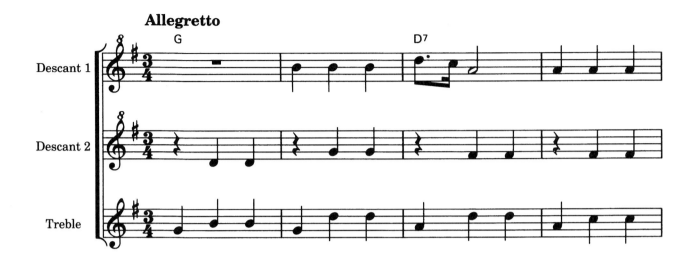

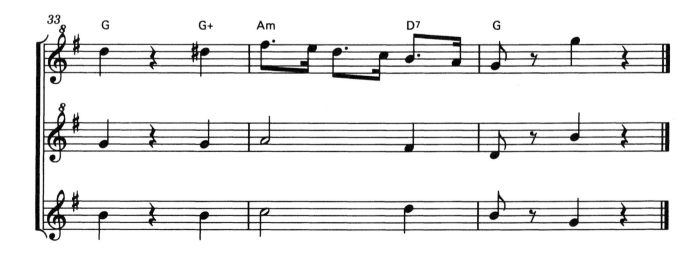

Rondo (K.213)   Mozart

Allegro moderato

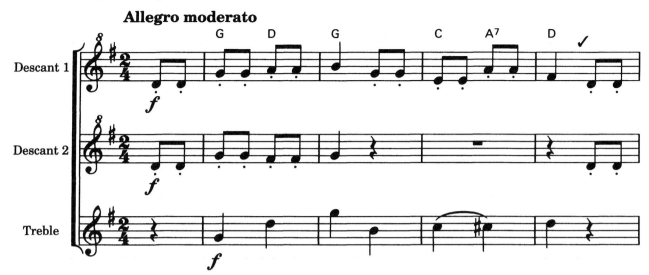

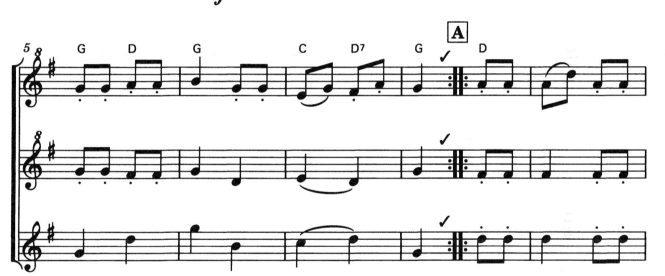

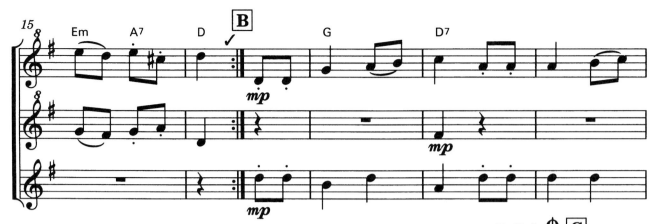

Da Capo al Coda

Beckett Blues   Pitts

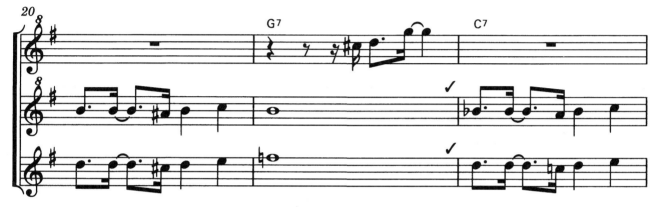

13

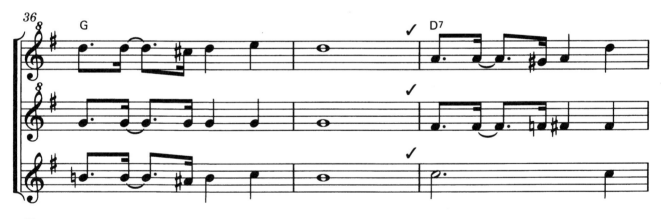

14

Go Down, Moses   Spiritual

Not too fast, with a swing

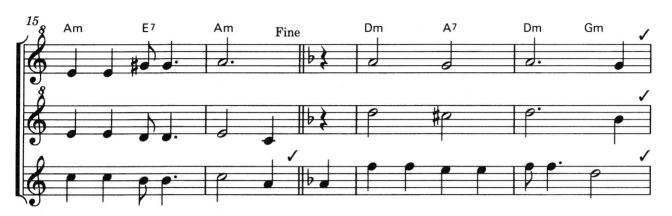

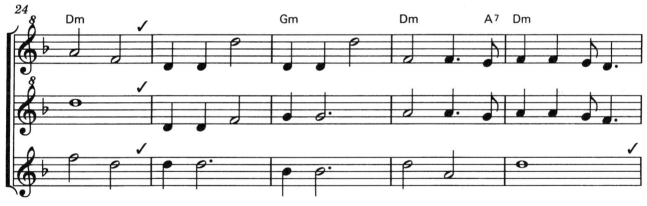

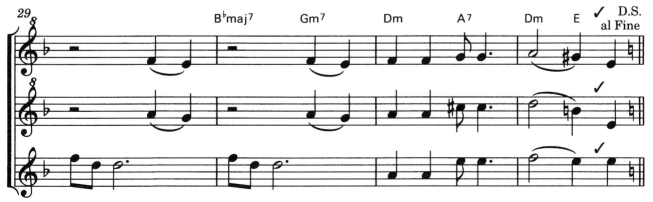

Christmas Spirituals

De Virgin Mary Had A Baby Boy

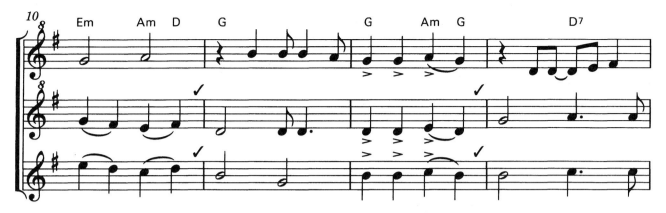

Rise Up Shepherd

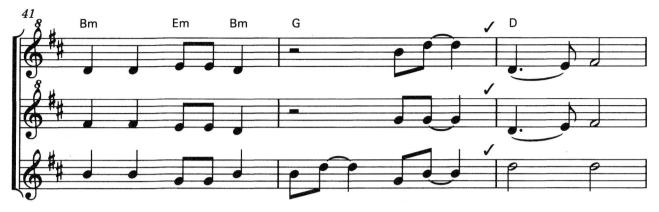

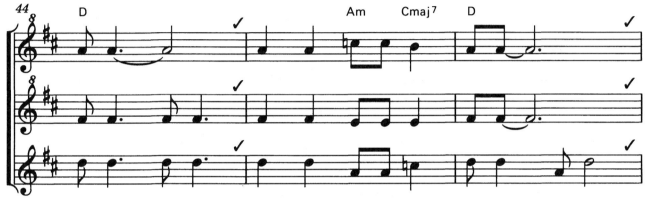

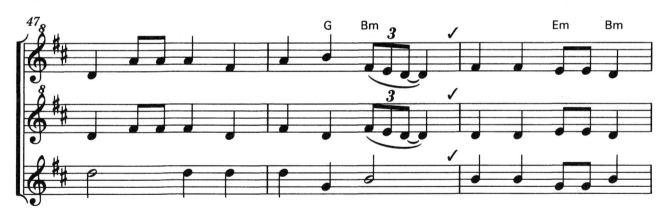

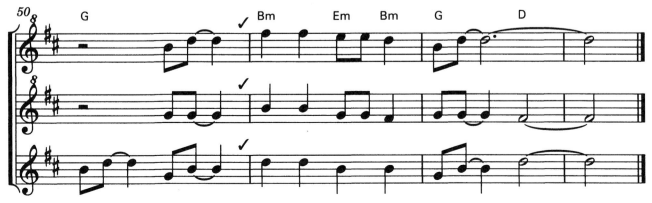

The Gospel Train   Spiritual

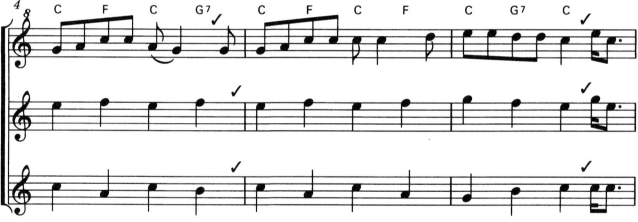

2 = Optional alternative fingering

St Anthony Chorale   Brahms

from Variations On A Theme Of Haydn

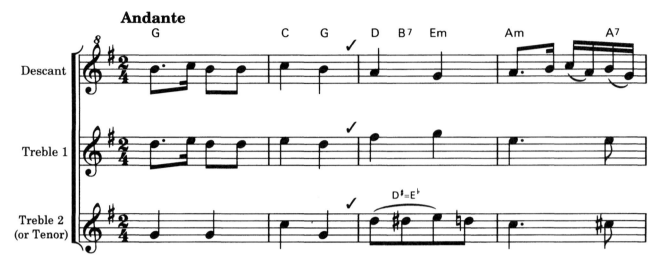

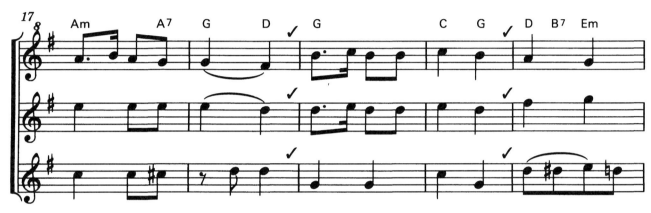

25

An Eriskay Love Lilt   Hebridean folk song

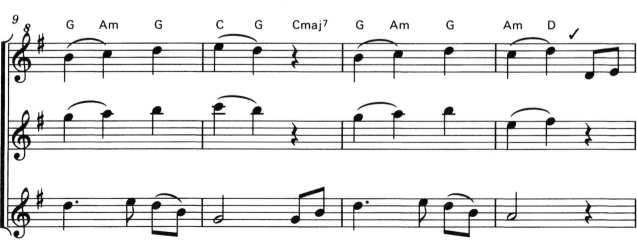

Yellow Bird Calypso

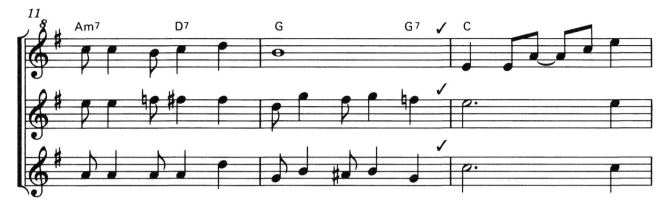

(first time continue overleaf)

To finish

Fine

29

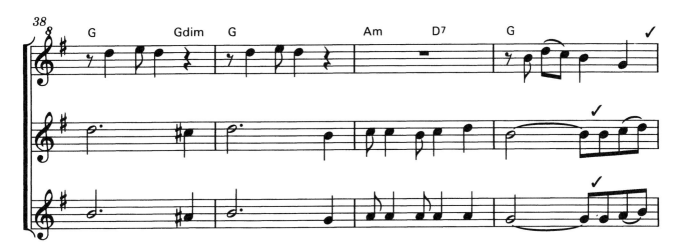

Las Heras Beguine   Pitts

2 = Optional alternative fingering

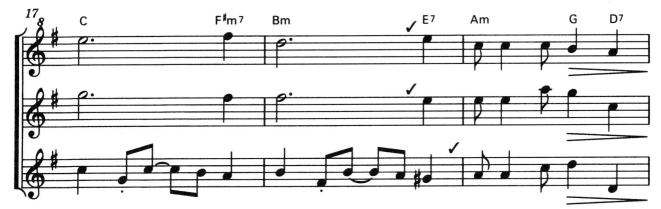

33

American Patrol   F.W. Meacham

2 = Optional alternative fingering

Calypso Carnival

2 = Optional alternative fingering

41

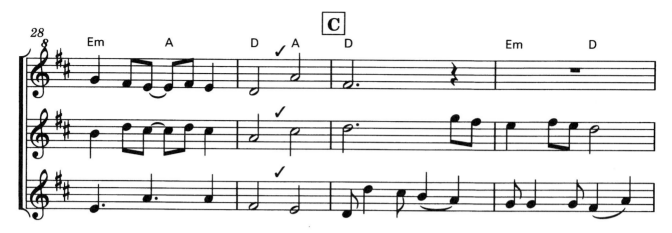

Scott Joplin in Concert

Peacherine Rag

Fingering Chart
English (Baroque) Fingered Recorders

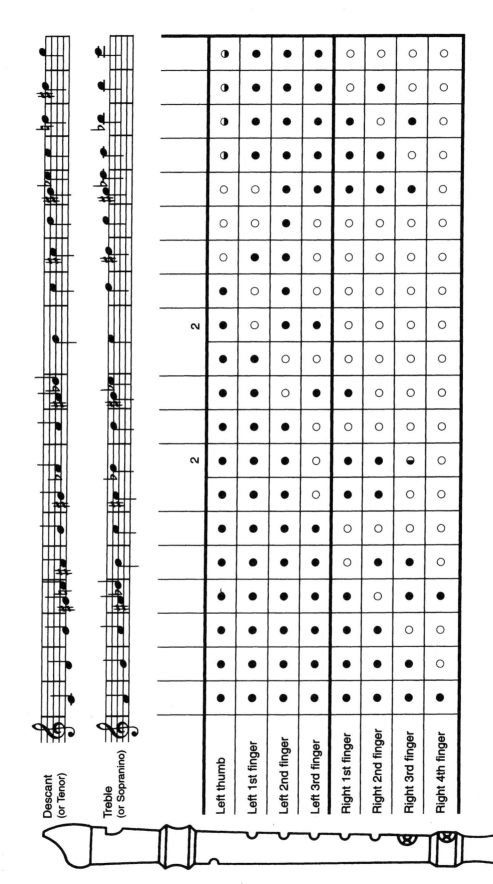

Descant (or Tenor)

Treble (or Sopranino)

| | Left thumb | Left 1st finger | Left 2nd finger | Left 3rd finger | Right 1st finger | Right 2nd finger | Right 3rd finger | Right 4th finger |

○ Open hole
● Closed hole
◑ Partly closed hole
2 Alternative fingering